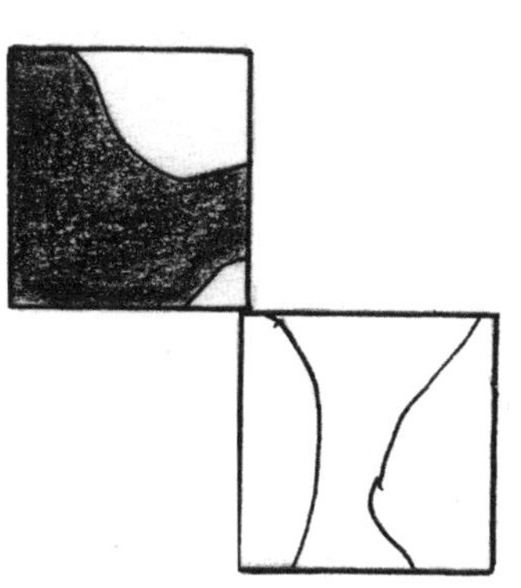

Mapmaker *of* absences

Mapmaker of absences

Maria M. Benet

Sixteen Rivers Press

Acknowledgments

Many thanks, with deep gratitude, to the Warren Wilson community of writers and the poets of Sixteen Rivers Press for their encouragement, support, and generosity.

Special thanks to Anne Berkeley for widening the circle of poets across the Atlantic, to Stephen Dodson for his help with Latin phrases, and especially to Rhonda Hammer and Robin Mansell for their friendship and inspiration.

Grateful acknowledgment is made to the following publications, in which these poems first appeared:

in·tense: "On the Road to Greenbrae"
Pearl: "Winter White"
Penumbra: "Instability," "Recovery"
Poetry: "Recursion"
Prairie Fire: "Quae Amissa, Salva"
Wellspring: "Incident," "A Romance of Roses"

Published by Sixteen Rivers Press
P.O. Box 640663
San Francisco, CA 94164-0663
www.sixteenrivers.org

Library of Congress Control Number 2004098910
ISBN 0-9707370-8-4

Cover and book design: EudesCo. | www.eudesco.com
Cover and interior artwork: Richard Rozen, *Untitled,* 2004

for my family

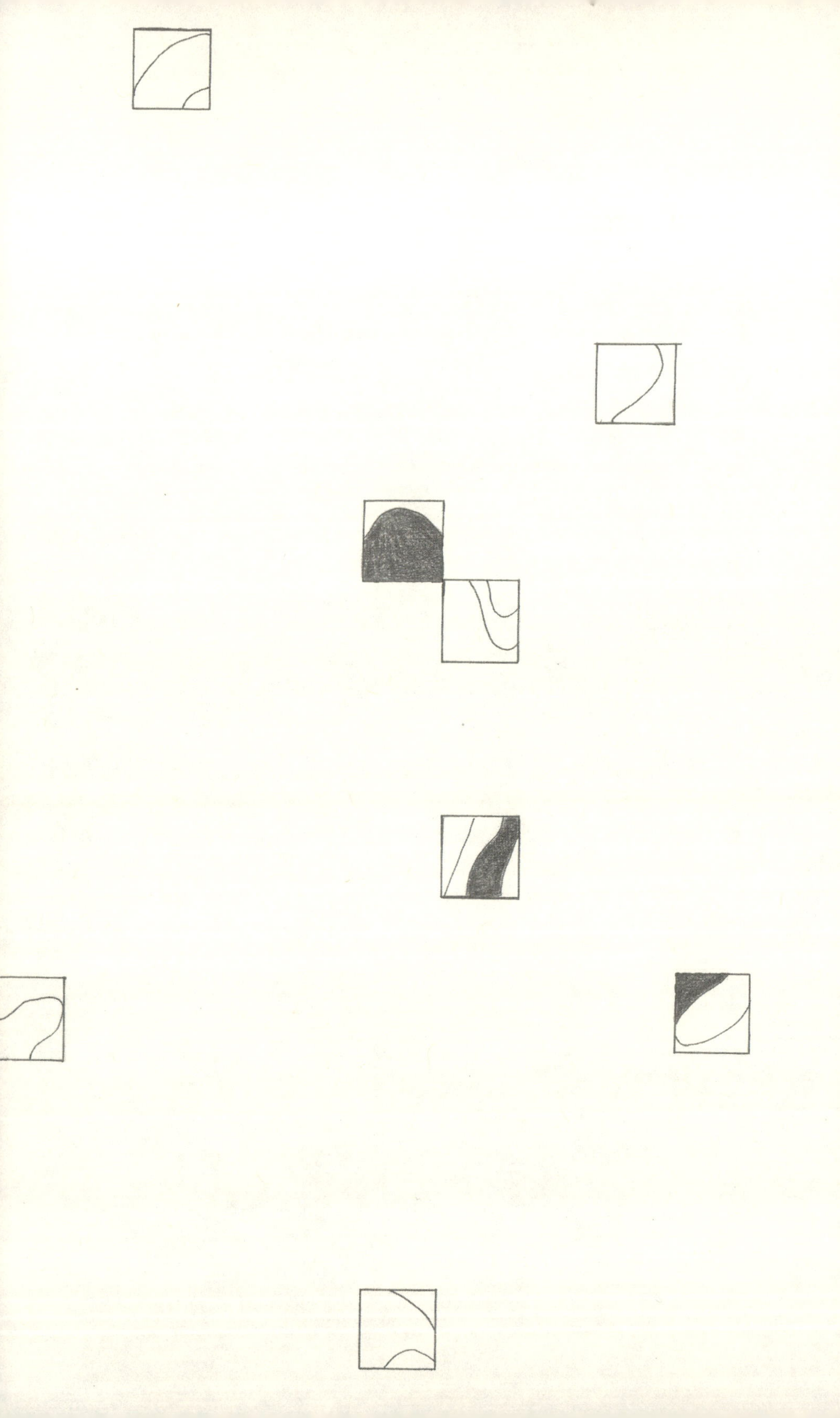

wresting pleasure from the dead calm

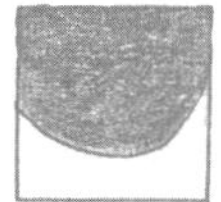

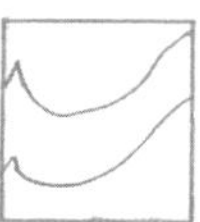

California Littoral

    —a wedding dress
       satin, trimmed with lace and beaded with artificial pearls
    —a check for $1,800
       endorsed in illegible writing
    —a full bottle of Prozac
       topped with cotton
    —a microwave oven
       made in Japan

The sand is a slack accountant who keeps
a cluttered ledger of losses and gains—

Perhaps in the surf
off the coast of Mendocino,
already breathless, a girl
slips out of her wedding dress,
long after she tells herself
it is better to be remembered
as the bride of the sea
than a landlocked wife;
or, perhaps in Cabo San Lucas,
someone else, a woman of means,
already a wife of many years,
does not want to be like a moon,
married to the inscrutable night,
so she tosses her mothballed dress,
that molted shell of promises.

For whatever it takes, the sea makes payment—

In permanent ink a check runs aground.
Services rendered. Debts canceled.
The price of a dress. A ticket

to a moonlit place that wears
the exact gloss of a photograph.

So, this is romance, the oasis
in a desert of waves. Someone
is stranded. It takes a check
to get home, to leave it behind.

Without Prozac, someone is
someone else tonight.
In Mendocino, Cabo San Lucas,
the air is stirred, roused, turned
to sound—*I, I*—the sea comes in
to meet the bluff of words, *do, do;*
a man or a woman on the brink,
between sea and land, moving
like a ship secured in a bottle, forever
in between.

I, I, the flares dim in the spray,
am, am still speaking as if
in tongues, Babel's dust
churns in the current of tides—

and the Japanese microwave oven, bobbing
in the blues of breakers, remains
itself, on a passage from shore
to sea and back again.

Standing-Water Habitat

Engines shut off, we drift on the surface.
Above us, a clear sky, the image
of a pristine lake.
Now and then, we speak
like limnologists checking on the health
of aquatic grasses,
bringing up whatever grows
in the shallow zones of memory.
Below us, the well-chilled depths—

I tell you that in Lake Baikal,
the world's oldest and deepest lake,
the candlefish is all mouth.
Imagine the void encased in scales—

And you tell me that lakes are scars,
vestiges of catastrophic events, drowned
meadows, starting over
in the frenzy of plankton.

We watch the man in a stiff black wetsuit
on his jet ski as he slams repeatedly
into miniature waves he makes
with each turn, wresting pleasure
from the dead calm.

On the horizon, a jet fighter
practices war maneuvers, laces
the sky with threads spun
from burned-up fuel.
Across the submerged meadow,
grasses bend in shifting currents.
The child that will be born to us,
all mouth, the cast of desire,
turns and turns.

The Queen of Romania

You just don't know, she says
in an English haunted by inflections
of a seldom-spoken language,
what it is like to do without.

Well, ask her children then, go ahead—
that's a dare. O grande dame of rococo
sorrow! Look, she wears black
visions borrowed from dead Greeks—

The queen of Romania, that's who
she thinks she is. Wearisome
the way this dame bores
her children, two plump pods

of a future she cannot fathom—
Marie of Romania, *regina aetheri,*
and her entourage of half-formed ideas,
picking over confections baked from books

she barely understands. At her feet
a wreath of weeds—*something somethings,*
she mumbles in her hackneyed Latin
to the child making the offering,

while the other, the one who hates his brother,
in the bat of an eye, flings the offending gift
out of sight. *The wind blew them away,*
honey, she tells the aggrieved one.

Tragedienne of swings and seesaws, I ask you,
what wind? Where you live,
there is always the heat, that ponderous
dead calm of August.

Orpheus . . .

homage to Rilke

At loose ends on a holiday weekend
in the long afternoon
he goes out, aware of things
missing in the cinnamon
parcel of wilderness in the slough
between two small towns. On the path,
men jog, girls pass him on roller skates,
and the old are asleep in wheelchairs.
Where are the wives? He asks . . .

He would like to show his own wife
the magnolias unburdened of a summer
of leaves, the bareness a brief interruption
in the stream of flowers—a recess, like grief.
Look, he says to no one in particular,
the world is full of things
unbecoming themselves:
egrets on the lattice of branches,
strewn about like old-fashioned
handkerchiefs—all whiteness
in the water's dark mirror—
sunsets at night's edge
charming the dull rubber
of discarded bicycle tires
into the gesturing flash
of retreating snakes . . .

What can change her, bring her back
as she was, his wife
who now stands in the kitchen,
a veil of steam on her glasses, the breath

of golden squash and plump turkey,
a small haven in the oven—

She is forever home in the house,
loosened in its rooms as she moves
from one small crisis to another:
a cup of juice spilled, a favorite toy
claimed by the depths of the couch.

Above him the last light of the day
and a circle of gulls with their querulous
chords—and he, at the path's head,
still looking back.

An Italian Romance

Ah, love . . . Volterra
and its brooding cliffs
already behind us.

In Florence, when you turn to me,
I say there is too much light here—

The sun is a giant cracked egg;
in its yolk even a single geranium
on a terrace forested with antennae
has the look of an old masterpiece.

You are in love.
The smile on your face is familiar,
as if the years of marriage have been nothing,
as if this were the beginning.

This time, I know you are taken
by the wind in the olive trees.

You see the artful light, obvious
blood-red geranium in the earthen pot,
the sun played back in a basket of lemons.

I can't seem to get enough of sunflowers
in late September: brittle stalks,
rigid leaves, heads bent
and facing the ground, the dark roots.

A Natural Argument

1. Premise

Had I not seen the fig trees in Italy,
trunks jutting from stone walls,
I could believe this sapling
in my garden is something special,
an embodiment of will, evidence
of the unseen, the way
it burst through the concrete
steps to the lawn—

So now this: my postulating garden scene,
these steps and a bare suggestion
of figs ripened into the deep blue substance
of hope. Could this be true—
that only a strict confinement of roots
yields the sweetest fruit?

2. Non Sequitur

Summer afternoons, they sit on the deck,
like this—it seems
they have been doing this
for years, he reading the paper,
and she always wanting to speak,
so when he raised his voice
to ask her if she was
happy, she was speechless.

Then, because the afternoon was long,
because the sun's warm indifference
would go on for many more hours,
she turned to him, but kept her eyes
on the small fig tree splitting
the concrete steps at the garden's edge,
and she said: "How could I be otherwise?"

A Romance of Roses

If I believed love could last forever,
I would have only one story to tell,
that of the man from France I saw on the news,
who loved his wife the way Romeo loved Juliet,
the way Tristan was beholden to Iseult.

I wonder if you can love me beyond all
words, if you could keep my room
the way the man from France has kept his wife's:
robe over wooden chair, slippers
by the unmade bed, and, on the dresser,
a forest of jars: creams and unguents.

I wonder if you believe in having always
the same wife by your side, the way
the man in France still does:
certain of the cure that will raise
a dead wife, he keeps her body
in a nearly empty basement,
in a freezer blanketed with roses,
shadows of his love unpent . . .

I wanted to tell you about love in France,
but when I called out, my voice
wouldn't carry to the other room,
so I fell asleep, certain in the dark
that you would try your very best,
because of your kindness,
not to disturb me, or wake me
later, when you'd join me in our bed.

Half an Hour

The poet Cavafy knew this kind of alchemy:
a life of visions fashioned from
the mud of words and a gracious stranger's pity—
the pleasures of art and proximity.

All of a sudden, hands, where there could be none,
the imagined pleasure of touch as if it were flesh
and not the dense blue vapor of longing.
It happened to me, but not in a bar as romantic

and terrible as Cavafy's. We were talking,
and in the late summer sun on the lawn's edge
we made a single shadow. Nothing will come of it, though
your words touched me, surely as if they had been hands.

Yet the memory of that half hour—your proximity,
the sun's accidental trick, the way I wanted you—
these stay, weighing me down like flesh,
dense, as is your absence.

In Transit

Now you are in mid-air, and below
the lakes of land break up
a continent of clouds; the fields,
shallow gashes in the white expanse,
the lusterless grass, worn patches
in the fur of the old retriever,
the one that loses sight of the stick
as soon as it leaves your hand.

Up here, freedom, like a dog's dream
rushing through the muscles of his leg,
memories of play. You are
between the place you left
and your destination. Your marriage,
the familiar hide—love
like an airborne stick,
flying out of sight.

Incident

I saw them, the man and woman,
under the great elm, out of reach,
lost in talk. I envied them
their small reef of shade
in the heat of summer,
and whatever else was
between them, when I caught
the way he reached out
to distract a persistent bee
from its course to her arm,
and how gently he brushed away
the danger of a sting.

Eclogue, Minor

Relics of a summer's barbecues:
ashes in the blackened chalice of the grill,
barnacled dust on the faded plastic flora
forever in bloom on cushions lodged
deep in the receptacle of loungers,
and at the patio's edge,
beyond the railing,
the wind's light turn
in a mix-up of branches,
the olive's silvery burn,
from which a jay
flies out, an abrupt blue.

Odysseus, Home

He finds her in the garden,
shears in gloved hands,
doing something to roses
he does not remember planting.

When he tells her it's over,
the long hours, the daily commute,
she drops the shears: "Never mind,
we'll fix the house, or take up golf."
A confusion of roses, a scented
Greek chorus, comes apart at her feet.

Like a great empty hall,
the garden is silent,
the clamor of voices quelled.
He picks up the fallen shears,
she gathers the roses. They stand
apart and overcome by longing.

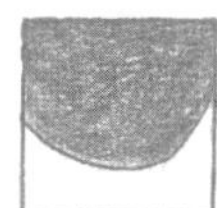

still within sight from the house

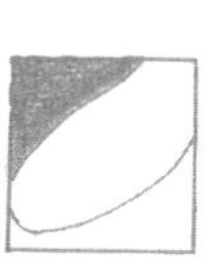

Baby Talk

Sweet risings,
the yeast of a child's breath,
mama, ama, ma...
How he likes you still,
yesterday's flour
in tomorrow's stale bread.

Unbleached grain of desire ...

So you speak, straight
and slender Pez, dispenser of
Sugar, honey, child of mine...
Sweet, sweet candy floss,
warp and woof of crystal
filaments spun to fluff.

Crisscrossing his brand-new teeth,
the grille of small cavities ...

And the ever-helpful dentists who offer
plastics, that which may seal
all cracks, openings.

Conviction

Even as we split the wood
I had no doubt
it was God's voice I heard
as the axe cleaved
limb from tree,
Take your son...

Even as I stacked
the twigs and branches
for the burnt offering,
uncoiled the mound of rope,
I had no doubt
it was God's voice
I must have heard,
Your son...

Even as I saw the eyes of my son
in the flare of the clean blade
of the knife, I had no doubt
it was God's own voice,
which brought me this far.

Then, when God's angel
came from nowhere and
called out: "Abraham,
Abraham, do not lay
your hand on the boy,"
when I saw the ram,
eyes glazed with death,
and those of Isaac bewildered,
when I felt the ram's warm
blood on my hands, and my son
turned away without so much
as a word, I knew then,
I had nothing, nothing
that wasn't doubt.

Isaac

Such drama: the gathering
of wood in a desert,
the uncoiling of rough rope,
then, the crude knife . . .
Abraham and that old business
of sacrifice—a glint of awe
in the raised blade,
then your reprieve:
salt in the bloodied wool of a ram.

Twice a week now, the ritual:
my son skips on one foot
across the worn diamonds
in the threadbare carpet, and I,
buffered in the hum of white noise,
thumb through the pages of magazines
that spill advice, from unruly curls
to overactive boys. Behind the door,
my boy and the good doctor
in a thicket of words.

Here, there is no scarcity of wood,
no one is handing me the rope,
no unearthly voice commanding
I take up the knife,
no bloody ram . . .

The Performance

No longer six, not yet seven, he
stands in the wings of an improvised
stage between the exit and the parents,
ready for the performance.

No curtains, no dimming of lights,
only the proscenium of library shelves,
rows of skinny volumes, spines
straight as bar codes,
and on the walls, paper windows
baring fields of Crayola flowers—
a domain of simple revelations.

Later, the teachers say
they are so proud of him,
a job well done. For ten minutes,
he was something definite,
his every gesture predictable,

a conductor on an imaginary train
heading for the polar expanse.
I saw the icy landscape coming
closer—at first, only a mirror
image caught in the flat pools
of his gaze while he explored the sea
of faces, mine among them.

I raised my hand to him, as in a wave,
and his own hand went up, like a flag,
then came his voice, something tinny
but loud and clear as he spoke
his one given line: "All aboard..."

Blood from the Stone

Not far from the row of houses
and their slow-afternoon hush,
not far from the burnished lawns,
a group of boys gather, and one by one,
throw stones at the birds' nests.
Among the trees, the air is charged,
swelling with boyish laughter.

Not far from the boys,
an intermittent swarm of birds,
numerous parents,
rend the air as they dart
between branches
through the light of nests.

Newly sociable, filled with pride,
my son, you who are among the boys
at wood's edge, still within sight
from the house, what can I say
to you in the light
of so much silence?

Nil Admirari

To wonder at nothing
—Horace

Since you ask, an angel,
my son, is everything
you and I are not. An angel
lives where we don't—
Imagine the abyss, or a black hole
the size of a pin, with an appetite
for matter. That's the angel:
everything, the meaning of legends,
loose ends, irrelevance,
life's mess, the tightly wound curls
around your forehead, everything and
everything else beyond habit's reach—
including fear's disproportioned renderings,
still life winged, beating
against the hole of words,
a way to speak of nothing . . .

Matins

... for as long as it takes
the relentless coming and going of a sun
on the other side of the drawn drapes
to undo time in the sliver-framed photograph,
to wash away the bright sheen of children's clothes—
oh, but the faces still so familiar, the younger one's chin
not yet his own, the older one's almond eyes,
an easy happiness, already like a souvenir ...

... this is what she sees first thing
every morning, long after her husband takes
the children to school. This what she says:
Today I will change everything, open the drapes,
let the light take whatever it claims.

Every morning this resolution
before she goes into the kitchen;
then, the morning paper, the litany
of disasters, planes gone down, trains
thrown off course—her day begins
with coffee, toast, and the pleasure
of knowing, without a doubt, what comes next.

Winnowing

Patient for resurrection
in the dust of some
secondhand shop,
your clothes, long outgrown,
folded in the plastic vault
of stacked boxes.

Before words wrought distance
between us, you
in my arms. At night,
summoned, I listened
to your cries, the sledge
in time's quarry—

Now to hold your baby blue jumper
and see on its lavender-shaded front
a great city's skyline
stitched in black, stone-blind
windows on cloth.

Root

. . . whereas trees have roots,
men have legs and
are each other's guests.

He asks in a voice
light as a stiletto's flash:
When you come home
this time, you won't ever
go away again?

In the heart's clay,
blood draws
cuneiforms of poppies.

A frieze of stalks
on the tongue's field,
and the sickling wind:

No, my son, I won't
go away again—
when I come home.

wager of spring

Incomplete Requiem

1. Kyrie

I wish I could write something splendid
about death, but my father had been dying
for years. By the time he was buried,
we had covered every angle of parting:
words, hugs, unmanly tears. Like children
dawdling at night, we had lingered
in doorways trying to stretch the day.
In the caverns of his sick robe, I have heard
too many times my voice and the echo
of my stale lines: "You'll be fine,
you'll pull through, don't you always?"
And after a few years, this way of speaking
was almost a chore, like waiting in line
for bread in lean times, wondering
if it would be all gone when my turn came,
nothing but empty shelves.

2. Requiem aeternum

There is a photograph of me
taken by my father at the cemetery.
I am wearing a loose sweater, his,
and my teenaged face is appropriately
solemn. I am leaning against the headstone,
against the names of grandparents
I have never known. At the bottom,
my father's name freshly engraved
in bright gold letters and the date
of his birth—that of his death
still missing. That I should forget
the year he died and remember only
the blank after the dash . . .

But that day in the cemetery, the air
was lush with the scent of chrysanthemums
and candle wax. Between the graves, on paths

wide enough for parades, old women sold gingerbread.
It was All Hallows' Eve, and we were
still together. We lit candles
and watched the crowd, the living
and the dead in a blaze of light.

Budapest Gothic

The trees are leafless, the street
in so much black rain, habitually bleak,
and the buildings, repositories of dreams,
rise on ambition laid to waste,
but in the cracks between the polished stones
there are signs of life,
cigarettes smoked to the bitter end.

And the women I used to know, how they stand
by the windows, plump shoulders curled in,
tongues syncopating the ballad of sighs;
but in the rooms, between polished furniture
there are signs of life,
pictures of saucy daughters, absent,
cracks on the hard shell of expectations.

Me, I left with her motherly blessing.
Here, the garden is blooming, like my house.
There are the drought-tolerant trees,
the furniture to withstand stormy kids.
And here, late in the season, among the flowers,
signs of her life: weeds, small clouds,
dark openings and cracks in the splendid light.

For Demeter

You kept me sheltered, always the flower,
nearly past the time of fruit,
teaching me nothing about the seasons.

To love him, I ask you, is it the same
as going under? In your vocabulary,
in the filigreed speech of petals,

is there a word for what I feel?
Up there, in the meadow of your hands,
you were so certain nothing could be lost.

How did this happen then, you ask me:
your bit of garden gone wild, your flower bent
on undoing itself, talking tough

in the slang of seeds hitting the ground,
taking refuge in the subtext
of hell, that language of descent

spoken by every flower gone to seed.
Can you understand my hunger,
the desire for new words?

Were you not here once?
Were you not like me, a wager of spring,
betting the seeds in your mouth?

Childhood

A long time ago, when I was ten,
I wore a red dress embroidered
with the weave of tiny white flowers
stiff from the sun
of slackened clotheslines.

In my red dress,
I stood with my mother
on the balcony of our rooms
while my father kept
adjusting his camera.

With one hand on the rusty rail,
the other safe in my mother's,
in the stupefying noon sun,
I watched the boys
climb over the fence, then disappear
in the weedy tangle
of the neighbor's garden.

And in the range finder,
my stricken face:
the wanderlust in me so strong,
it was hard
to distinguish from homesickness.

Blue Danube

You listen to waltzes on the radio,
your feet tap on the well-worn rug,
your eyes shadow a past—
the patterned turns
in illuminated halls
where lights aggrandized
the slightest of gestures.

Then came the war, the war
of wars—your youth in halls,
the shattered chandeliers,
dollops of tears, scattered
constellations in shards of glass . . .

and a thicket of guns, the march of boots,
that measured beat in my inured ears.

Winter White

Years since my last real winter,
my father up from bed, standing
by the radiator and the mild fever
I had borrowed to be alone with him

inside the soothing twirl of snow
drifting over his flimsy frame.
How he seemed to move toward me
from across the steady banks of snow,

as if he were roaming on the other side
of the window. How he fluttered then,
his hands, the wings of chilled birds
fallen from the icy nest of his breath,

and his face, unable to thaw
in his daughter's whimsical fever,
was bleak inside its layers of white.
How he drew from the space between us

the visions I could not see in the waves of heat
rising from the radiator; how I stood there,
like a bulb, planted for spring. Around us,
flurries of words and snow, enormous floods on ice,

inside each flake of crystalline snow,
a numb season, my father's faith
in filial love held solid
in the blanks of winter white.

Quae Amissa, Salva

What has been lost is safe.
—Latin saying

That summer, the heat was plenty enough—
stillness and small sorrows in fields of wheat
across the great Hungarian plain. I took a train
back to the mild hills of my Romanian childhood town,
where my father was at home. In those days,
he was always at home.

"I can't get up," he said. "There is still the daily news,
the papers, and the radio. As long as I can laugh, now
and then, I suppose, it's all right."

He was nestled on his pillow,
so I couldn't tell if he really was unbroken,
as he claimed to be. He was sick—
but then, I never knew him when he was well.

Above his head, on the wall, something new: a small cross.
A couple of rough sticks and a generic Jesus,
the kind you'll find in the plump hands of husbandless women
who stand on church steps with listless priests,
talking about the miracle of Lazarus,
long after he went back to the comforts of the dead.

My mother was away, safe as thunder,
and there was no priest in my father's neighborhood,
no easy relief, no molten metal to set
hard as that homely Jesus in his smooth cast on the wall.

We had tea with milk,
a British custom of which we knew little—
he from books, and I from wishes to please him—
but which we nevertheless observed.
We talked, or rather, I bragged. I was
going places, and he thought
this was as it should be.

"The war, the last war, was terrible,"
he said, "never again."

I was still a child then, and believed
his heaven of pale saints was
as close as America, and his new Mass
in that war's aftermath, a custom,
like tea with milk, and not the memorial
for his forfeited Shabbat.

"You lived," he said, "or died
by the name of your God. But you die,
regardless."

In those days, my father had a cat,
a stray that slept on his bed.
Her breaths filled the room like the ticking of a clock,
a relentless beat without a tune. I was still a child then,
and it seemed there was little else I could do.

We watched the sun, or rather what remained, blaze
dull against the fence. My father fell asleep, and I left.
When I closed the door, I saw his hand sink into the cat's fur.
There was his labored breath, and outside, a world
between the changing light, ragged edges everywhere—
and somewhere in America, in the lifting mists, the day begins.

Harvest

It's what an immigrant mind makes
from memory's flour:

The men, wearing broad-brimmed hats,
move across the field, wielding scythes.
The language they speak is a low, dark hum,
like a distant gathering of bees
claiming the horizon.

The child is barefoot—
mimicking the men, she swings
her stick at tall nettles, poppies.

The women, dressed in black, bring soup
in tiered tins, bread in stiff linens.

The child is mute as she sits
under the whorled branches of an oak.
She dips her piece of bread in milk
and listens to the women's singsong:

That boy's club foot, surely
the devil's kiss. That girl's wide hips,
a cradle for many children. Future's boneyard
in every body. The world in the noonday sun,
a picture book; every page is more
and less than what it is.

By late afternoon, the field is but stubble,
straw has been sheaved into effigies of huts,
the men have wiped clean their scythes,
and the light, which has withheld shade
from the fields, gives way to dark.
The child is asleep.
In the cool well of a lap, words tumble, sink
like pebbles in pooled water.
The child's dreams are a tangle of stars
sprouting green skies. To her hunger
there is no end.

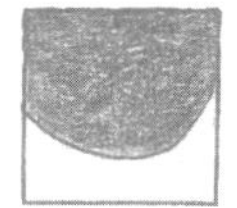

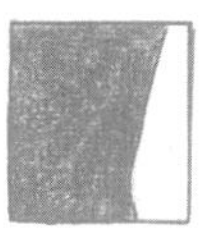

the end of daylight saving time

Impersonations of the Muse

They are all men now, the boys I used
to know . . . but I remember the rustle in the step
of the one who turned the stillness of my girlish room
upside down, and how I fell into his arms, swaying,
everything succumbed to wind. All his kisses
left me wanting.

Athwart, he comes, years later,
sashaying and dapper
with words he turns into pulp,
inclement lexicon, his love a ruse,
he thumbs through my soul—

My body, no intaglio,
poses no risk to him,
he who now speaks as if I were
de-embered. He tells me of girls,
foundries of wishes in the refine
of bright hair, the windy lisp
in the scribble of their steps,
winsome gavotte—his feet conscripted,
he is swaying, swaying . . .

Remainder, I am the theater
without opening night, the dress
rehearsal for the folly of his voice;
swaying, everything swaying, I am
stilled. His lips are
without ligatures—kerned
desire leaves me wanting nothing
more when he lets go of my mouth.

Winter Solstice

for B. R.

We are snowless here
in the temperate country—
unlike the place you call home,
where every now and then,
after the fall's devastation,
the first snow's fresh linen
swaddles the ground—the bared
fields, as well as the gravid barn.

Here, only the thinned fog
over green ridges, ghost to white
on the periphery of the hour
between night's hold
and morning's repair.

That, and against the windowpane
December's lost bee,
a jarring hymn of wings,
welcomes the season.

Spring Rites

The gardener is out there
with a new set of clippers, shearing
the ornamental pear. Somewhere between
a stunted tree and an overgrown bush,
it grows out of control in the rainy season.
For months, the woods in my window.
Now the gardener is so pleased. No more
dead wood, the excessive zeal of buds
nipped back to bark. Oh, the light;
nowhere to hide. Even the linen blind
I pull over the bare glass is white,
inscrutable like a blizzard.

Trees at Dawn

for Simone Weil

In the vaulted spaces
that bracketed the trees,
I saw her body's hollow,
shaft to thread of light
that bolts her to the firmament—

Trees, she once wrote,
are rooted in the sky,
seeing how they live by light—
Behold the brilliance,

its chiseled periphery, a halo
that obliterates the blueprint
of random stars riveting
night's dark in place.

On the Road to Greenbrae

after Eugenio Montale's "On the Road to Vienna"

The shopping malls, all pink
candy floss and crisp gray Styrofoam,
shaded strips of asphalt
and a few cars, dappled here and there
with August's fierce sun.

We emerged from stores
in clouds of shopping bags.
Pastel-toned canvas banners
loosely anchored to steel posts
surged with wind, luffing, as if
they were meant to sail . . .

A rhythmic pounding against
the coreless posts, and from the hills,
out of a distant yard,
a leaf blower brayed, whined to a halt—

sole familiars in the vast parking lot.

Roses

I don't know where Rilke found
those carefree roses whose countless folds
could, forever, hold entire summers
within their scented cores. The roses
I bought at the farmers' market
had twelve pink buds—perfect
if perfection is a matter of symmetry.

After three days of cautious flowering,
after each petal had bent itself back
with equal force, the roses began to wilt
in concert. What vast inner lakes
or bright heavens may have graced
the center of those blossoms remains
a mystery enfolded within this precision
of a synchronized collapse.

Iridescence

She rises from her beach chair
in the still-warm sand.
Her shadow lengthens,
its shade turns solid,
like stone. Standing at the edge,
facing all that water, in a world
about to go dim, she is astonished
by the light that binds the horizon—
twilight, burning brighter
than all the high noons
of a sun she can remember.

Disenthrallment

Like a bird that flies into the window,
mistaking the image in the stretch of glass
for open territory, he lifts himself on wings
of spindled bone . . . His legs fold
under him—and out of his reach,
the makeshift urinal,
hooked into the nightstand's drawer,
that quaestor to dentures, hearing aid,
and bifocals whose thick bowls mirror
the expanse of glass on glass . . .
. . . what are these things to the boy
who remains inside the folds of skin, the flesh
like emptied rooms—and lately his mother's voice,
at dawn and dusk, like starlings in some old city park,
darkening lindens and sycamores.

Recovery

These ballet slippers,
size eight,
were fashioned from hog casings.
Opaque, yet translucent,
the way the world appears
in a wash of mist,
they hover under Plexiglass
in the nearly empty waiting room
of the oncology department.
From the body, illness,
given a pair of slippers, goes lightly
across the stage lit up by the vigors
and bents of hope,
never touching ground.

Triptych: Crossings

1.

When she wakes, she is river,
her bed, sodden unrest, the current
too fast for the paper armada
of hope in which her days tumble
through agitated foam, the mercurial
fall from boulder to boulder,
each outcrop an hour's halt,
and again, back in the water.
She is ungroundable—

2.

Landlocked, I watch
you slip through the river;
I am without rope,
nothing to cast, no line
to throw from where I stand,
steady in the day's habitual ground.

3.

The banks are littered with light,
the fishing is good for egret or man—
October's wind whips small hurricanes
between marooned cities
of driftwood and discarded cans.
In the marshland, this close to the bay
reeds cradle what the sea refused.

Days of Awe

What of the body? Weaned of flesh,
the skin, shroud to bones.
In the lashed raft of a bed,
your outline
a crudely stitched hem.

What of the mind? Filigreed spice box
to cinnamon and cloves.
The scent of other days turns
your thoughts
to bitter seeds in your mouth.

We bring you honey and apples:
May it be your will, we say to God,
to renew on us a good and sweet year ...
You turn away. To remember
is the kind of hope you
will not claim.

We begin the first blessing,
as we have each new year
and as we shall again
to remember the way
you turned from us.
What of us? Root ends
in night's dense loam.

The End of Daylight Saving Time

You hoard
grain in the silo
of an extra hour—
autumn's field, the crop
picked clean. Your hopes
on pegs, dumb clothes hung up
in the vestibule. The fire is out,
not gone. Black is the absence
of all light. In your mouth,
bread of ash and everything
that is *after*.

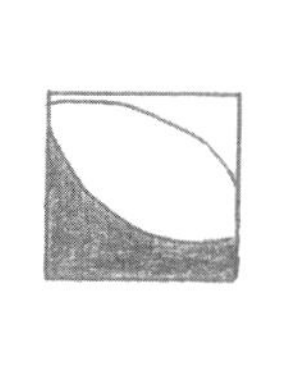

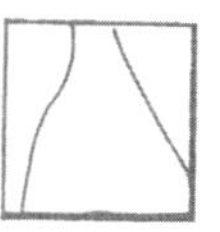

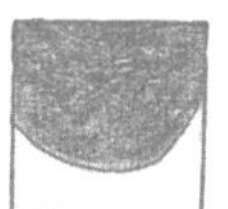

raft of words

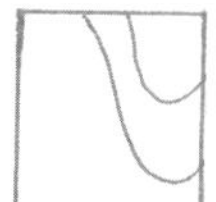

Polyglot

She keeps the name
of things in containers
labeled by the languages she once knew—
at least that's how she imagines
they will stay put, exact, and still
                    in her mind,
        that salted lighthouse—the name
of things, she keeps
in containers labeled by the languages
she knew once . . . at least
that's how she imagines—

        containers, the solid grid of their angles,
parceling tracts bound by treaties, the spaces
where dachas score the banks of the Dnieper, and in Dachau
a bush unleaves itself in light, aglow with dew, or
the moon over the Danube rises and falls
in the arch of her blue palm, the hold of her hand
        should she be able to grasp it—

        ár, are, Ararat—her ark is loaded
unsteady in the stream of amended vowels

        she imagines—that's how
at least she keeps the name
        of things she once knew
in all the languages
                    in her mind,
        that's how she imagines—
                        once she knew how.

Ghazal

Here is your mother's tender hand: a burden.
This comfort she bears has no end: a burden.

Over hills, new grasses cover their ancestors:
a green pitch of blades, the wind penned, a burden.

In your heart of painted Russian dolls I am forever
inside: my love a lessened brand, a burden.

Memory, the mapmaker of absences, tracing
vanishing steps—the fugitive friend, a burden.

When your health turns into a ripped garment, dreams
are tailors with needles poised to mend: a burden.

Bitter is my name in my father's ancient tongue;
on my mother's lips, joy conscripts my name: a burden.

Three American-Style Studies
of a Landscape Rendered Foreign

1. Cluj

after William Carlos Williams

Trunks by the door
blue and gold

obscured in dim light—
smell of dust—

Sun of early morning—
on the wood floor

a wood frame, the picture
missing, next to it

scissors are lying—and the
cavernous empty room

2. Autumn Begins in Cluj, Transylvania
    after James Wright

In the town square, whose name I forgot,
I imagine girls nursing verdant dreams of America,
and the spent walk of women who know better.
Over our heads, the rusted blank stare of King Mathias,
his statue a dream of heroes, fixed in the distance.

All those who stayed on are proud to be hungry.
Their relatives, far from home, in their new language,
do not know hunger or pride.

So, then,
dreams, ours and theirs, from afar grow full
like the harvest moon,
and pride, like dry leaves, falls to hunger's bare ground.

3. A Dish of Peaches in Cluj
   after Wallace Stevens

A peach is sweeter than any other
if its taste is the sun of years, the idea
of a peach, extravagant and plump
staked to the espalier of the tongue—

The peach was on a branch, the branch was
from a tree, and the tree grew
in a town that had a name
in three languages.

A peach is the sun in the faience of sky,
one noon in the bowl of hunger;
one boat on a sea without
the allure of tides—

The peach was enormous. It sat on the sill.
The window was one of many, the town
was one. It was the only one,
the one I left behind.

A peach is a word, and a word is the path
that winds around the appetite
like a tourniquet. *Pierscă, barack, Pfirsich.*
Which one is my one and only peach?

The peach is a fruit I ate yesterday.
It came from Chile or Peru, full of sun—
I did not know that any peach could ripen
into the sole peach of the tree in Cluj.

Recursion

A tomato I overlooked on the window ledge
remembers the hold of vine, the brace of ground,
and puts down roots inside its own flesh.

Halved under the blade of my knife,
the tomato unbinds its shoots, sends them
into an abyss of air and light—

Here at my desk I sit remembering,
putting down words far from the vine
of a native tongue, as if they could be roots,

each, like the tomato with its faith curlicued
in pale inward shoots, calling to itself,
back to the source of fruit.

Echo

A bridge of flowers,
the reach of tulip,
forget-me-not, poppy.
Suspension of bloom
across the gorge:

Downstream

the one world,
flooded plain
in the mouth. So much
water under the bridge. Over
the chattering flux,
an arc of sound

Echo.

Bolt of lightning
across night's well.
The shattering glow
that scatters
the script-
like cue of stones

Below.

Hydroelectric Complex

From the headbay of the reservoir
through the gate, rapids
halt in the penstock;
the turbine rotates,
and all is calm in the afterbay.

Along the banks of countless rivers,
and far into lands
that lie in night
(always, somewhere it is night)
lamps go on, one by one—

In spring, and always after a heavy storm,
at the crest of the spillway
a rush through the chute,
the roar—like a voice spared
the rotating blade of words, sound
untransformed—

Twitter of Dust

On the logged slope of the tongue,
the razed forest of consonant trees:
trunks in splinters, divided roots strewn
in a sludge of vowels.

The cleanup crew, a brash legion
of ciphers, dredges the ruts,
erects a scaffold lashed
by knots of weathered syntax.

Polished rivets of words
smelted from alien ore
spill from abundant tool chests;
littering the floor, they put forth

buds of light that flicker.
Soon it stands: the sound edifice
reassembled in the new language—
mortared sense, steeled music.

My tower, the gloss on ruins,
raised anew in the twitter of dust.

Instability

For he remembered that they were but flesh;
a wind that passes, and comes not again.
— Psalm 78:39

When the pious ones ask
the One to open
their lips so that they will
sing his praise,
there is nothing
to hold the wind—

In the wake of the exalted
surge of air drawn upward,
what remains is
space, emptied of air—
the downward slap of a wing
and burn in the lungs.

The One listens to
the wind; and the pious ones,
sheltered from gusts, sway
on rafts of words,
rudderless through
streams of blood.

Border Questions

What is a border?
Measure without distance,
the still-gleaming rock
in the dry riverbed,
distance without measure,
the stream gone past all beds,
rivers in the fields.

What is a border?
The calcified watermark, remembrance
of floods. The bone-dry trough
in burnt fields, the sentry of trees
on the horizon, the line
that keeps distance and measure
within reach.

What is a border?
The ark in your chambered heart
with its twin cargo, wonder and belief,
the scrolled tide of
an untethered conviction
that on the border
every brink is the core.

Notes

The epigraph of "California Littoral" is composed from
a list of items that were washed ashore on California's beaches,
as reported on the news one night in the late 1990s.

"Orpheus . . ." is a suburban response to Rainer Maria Rilke's
"Orpheus. Eurydice. Hermes."

Some of the images in the last stanza of "Odysseus, Home"
derive from Homer's *Odyssey*.

"Root": The epigraph is a quote found in an essay by George
Steiner in his collection *George Steiner: A Reader* (New York:
Oxford University Press, 1984).

"Polyglot": The word *ár* is a Hungarian homophone that covers the meaning of such unlikely cohorts as *flood, cost, awl,* and
punch, among others. The English verb *hold,* in its Hungarian
homophone equivalent denotes both *moon* and a measure of
land that is approximately 1.42 acres.

In the sequence "Three American-Style Studies of a Landscape
Rendered Foreign," the poems "Cluj" and "Autumn Begins in
Cluj, Transylvania" are modeled after "Nantucket," by William
Carlos Williams, and "Autumn Begins in Martins Ferry,
Ohio," by James Wright, respectively. The last poem in the
series, "A Dish of Peaches in Cluj," is a response to "A Dish
of Peaches in Russia" by Wallace Stevens.

 Sixteen Rivers Press is a shared-work, nonprofit poetry collective dedicated to providing an alternative publishing avenue for San Francisco Bay Area poets. Founded in 1999 by seven women writers, the press is named for the sixteen rivers that flow into San Francisco Bay.

Also from Sixteen Rivers Press:

difficult news, by Valerie Berry

Translations from the Human Language, by Terry Ehret

Snake at the Wrist, by Margaret Kaufman

After Cocteau, by Carolyn Miller

What I Stole, by Diane Lutovich

Sacred Precinct, by Jacqueline Kudler

No Easy Light, by Susan Sibbet

Falling World by Lynn Trombetta

Swimmer Climbing onto Shore by Gerald Fleming

San Joaquin * Fresno * Chowchilla * Merced * Tuolumne * Stanislaus * Calaveras * Bear
Mokelumne * Cosumnes * American * Yuba * Feather * Sacramento * Napa * Petaluma

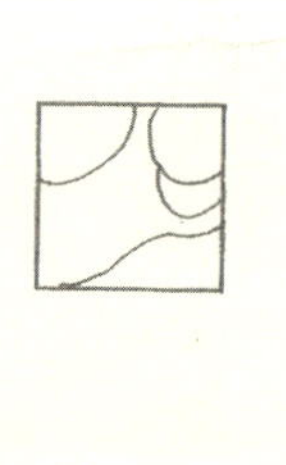

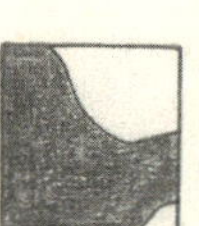

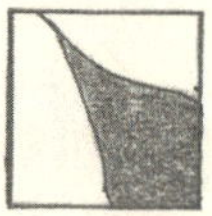